Bishop Burton College

T012912

BISHOP BURTON COLLEGE

T012912   16,487   ©

636.1

#352

HORSES
· SECOND EDITION ·

*A Guide to Selection,
Care, and Enjoyment*

HORSES

· SECOND EDITION ·

A Guide to Selection, Care, and Enjoyment

J. WARREN EVANS

Texas A&M University
College Station, Texas

W. H. FREEMAN AND COMPANY

New York

Library of Congress Cataloging-in-Publication Data

Evans, J. Warren (James Warren), 1938-
    Horses: a guide to selection, care, and enjoyment / J. Warren
  Evans. — 2nd ed.
      p.   cm.
    Bibliography: p.
    Includes index.
    ISBN 0-7167-1971-1
    1. Horses.   I. Title.
SF285.E933 1989
636.1 — dc19

88-23659
CIP

Copyright © 1981, 1989 by W. H. Freeman and Company

No part of this book may be reproduced by any mechanical, photographic, or electronic process, or
in the form of a phonographic recording, nor may it be stored in a retrieval system, transmitted, or
otherwise copied for public or private use, without written permission from the publisher.

Printed in the United States of America

3 4 5 6 7 8 9   HL   9 9 8 7 6 5 4 3 2